Caerleon Roman Fortress

Jeremy K. Knight BA, FSA

A History of Roman Isca

In Search of Isca

The traveller who comes to modern Caerleon, Arthur Machen's 'noble, fallen Caerleon on Usk', in search of the Roman legionary fortress of *Isca*, will find a small town of some 7,000 people, standing beside a crossing of the tidal river Usk, and not yet wholly swallowed up by the urban sprawl of nearby Newport. The early nineteenth-century stone bridge is the successor of Roman and medieval timber bridges, which had stood a little further up the river on the opposite side of the Hanbury Arms. The last of these earlier bridges largely collapsed in a memorable storm in 1772 and although patched up, it was eventually replaced on a new site. The older bridges stood on the line of the *via praetoria* — one of the main roads of the Roman fortress — where it led down to the river. In medieval and later times, merchant ships sailed from quays on the riverside at Caerleon to Bristol, to Ireland, and to Atlantic ports such as La Rochelle and Lisbon. For the Romans, who established their strategic base for the conquest of south Wales here in AD 74 or 75, the site offered major advantages when compared to that of their earlier legionary station some 8 miles (13km) up river at Usk. From a fortress near the mouth of the Usk, the legion could be readily supplied with food and munitions by sea. The new fortress was to bear the name of the river, *Isca*.

The Roman ruins at Caerleon have attracted travellers for at least eight hundred years. In 1188 Gerald of Wales, Giraldus Cambrensis, (d. 1223), on a recruiting tour for the Third Crusade, saw there 'a lofty tower, and beside it remarkable hot baths'. He also described buildings both within and without the walls, with underground passages and hypocausts. Gerald was in no doubt that these buildings were Roman. In contrast, in an entirely fictional epic, his contemporary, Geoffrey of Monmouth, identified Caerleon as the court of King Arthur. His *History of the Kings of Britain* proved so popular in the Middle Ages that Caerleon soon appeared as Arthur's court in medieval Welsh and French romances.

In 1405, a French expeditionary force in support of Owain Glyn Dŵr took time off to inspect the Roman amphitheatre, by then 'King Arthur's Round Table'. In the reign of Queen Elizabeth I (1558–1603), a topographer-poet told how:

> In Arthurs tyme, a table round,
> Was there whereat he sate:
> As yet a plot of goodly ground,
> Sets foorth that rare estate...

> There are such vautes and hollow caves,
> Such walles and condits deepe:
> Made all like pypes of earthen pots,
> Wherein a child may creepe.

> Such streates and pavements sondrie waies,
> To every market towne...

Thomas Churchyard, *The Worthines of Wales* (1587).

But by this time many of the impressive ruins seen by earlier visitors had vanished — robbed ('mooted up' was the local term) to build the houses of Caerleon. The one surviving tower of Caerleon Castle, next to the Hanbury Arms, is built almost entirely of Roman stones, as are almost all the older buildings in the town.

By the seventeenth century, travellers were recording Roman finds from Caerleon. These included coins, fragments of inscriptions and sculpture, and tiles marked with the legionary stamp, LEG II AVG, which confirmed that this was the fortress of the Second Augustan Legion.

Opposite: Caerleon Roman amphitheatre, known for many years as 'King Arthur's Round Table', was built close to the south-west defences of the Roman legionary fortress of Isca. The fortress was established by the Second Augustan Legion on the banks of the river Usk around AD 75, and the amphitheatre was built some fifteen years later.

The surviving thirteenth-century tower of Caerleon Castle, adjacent to the Hanbury Arms, is built of stone robbed from earlier Roman buildings within the fortress.

Although derelict, the remains of Roman Caerleon impressed medieval visitors and their grandeur may have equalled that of the baths at Hadrian's villa at Tivoli, near Rome, shown in this eighteenth-century engraving by Giovanni Battista Piranesi (1720–78). The eighteenth-century fascination with Roman antiquities inspired visitors to Caerleon to record inscriptions and to buy relics, but did not prevent the pillaging of stone from the fortress for building material (RIBA Library Photographs Collection, London).

Travellers' accounts from the seventeenth century and later mention finds of Roman antiquities from Caerleon. Stamped tiles, coins and fragments of inscriptions, like those depicted in this illustration from E. Donovan's Excursions through South Wales and Monmouthshire (London, 1805), provided confirmation that Caerleon was the site of the fortress of the Second Augustan Legion.

Most of these relics were either sold to visitors or lost, and Roman inscriptions were reused as building material or broken up to mend the roads. Eventually, John Edward Lee (1808–87), a Yorkshire businessman who had settled in Caerleon, persuaded local people to join him in building a museum to preserve such finds, which opened in 1850. Lee also founded the Caerleon (now Monmouthshire) Antiquarian Association to run the museum. In time however, its upkeep proved too much for a local society, and in 1930 the National Museum of Wales took over responsibility.

The old town of Caerleon occupied only a small part of the area of the Roman fortress, much of which was still open fields. However, the town was growing, and previously untouched parts of the buried remains were disappearing under modern housing. A start was made on the archaeological exploration of the fortress in 1908, when land that was to be used to extend the churchyard was excavated. Systematic rescue work, whereby parts of the fortress were excavated before they were

destroyed by building developments, began in 1926. A local excavation committee was set up on the initiative of the director of the National Museum of Wales, Mortimer Wheeler (1890–1976). Wheeler also persuaded *The Daily Mail* to sponsor the excavation of the Roman amphitheatre ('King Arthur's Round Table'), and to present the site to the then Office of Works (the predecessor of Cadw) as a national monument.

When a field in the western angle of the fortress, Prysg Field, came on the market as building land in 1927, the local excavation committee raised £2,500 to buy it. It was excavated by an archaeologist on the staff of the National Museum, Victor Nash-Williams (1897–1955). His work revealed a row of Roman barracks, which were also given to the Office of Works. Since then, there has been a 'rescue' excavation at Caerleon almost every year — save during the Second World War — until recent times, often in advance of housing development. More recently, geophysical survey has revealed the plans of buildings in areas

The Caerleon amphitheatre was excavated in 1926–27 by Dr R. E. M. Wheeler (later Sir Mortimer) and his wife, Tessa. During the work, huge quantities of spoil had to be removed, as seen in this 1927 view of work in progress. The site remains the most fully excavated amphitheatre of Roman Britain (© National Museum of Wales).

HISTORIC SITE FOR THE NATION.

BRITAIN'S BIGGEST ROMAN AMPHITHEATRE.

GIFT BY "THE DAILY MAIL."

EXCAVATIONS TO BE BEGUN.

We are able to announce to-day the conclusion of negotiations by which one of the most interesting Roman sites in Britain will be preserved, excavated, and handed over to the nation.

The site—at Caerleon, in Monmouthshire—is that of the largest Roman amphitheatre in the kingdom where in the days of the Cæsars gladiators fought and, according to tradition, Christian martyrs were put to death as they were in the great Colosseum in Rome.

The Daily Mail has now supplied funds to the Caerleon Excavation Committee to enable them to purchase this historic centre for the British people. Parts of the amphitheatre have already been found, and new excavations will be begun at about the end of the month which, it is hoped, will yield important discoveries.

Subject to the approval of the Office of Works, the amphitheatre, after it has been excavated under the supervision of Dr. R. E. M. Wheeler, Director of the National Museum of Wales, and placed as nearly as possible in the state in which it was when the Roman legionaries used it for their public games and shows, will be transferred to the Office of Works as a permanent national monument for the enjoyment and the instruction of the public.

Pictures in the Back Page.

Far left: Wheeler persuaded The Daily Mail *to sponsor the excavations, and the newspaper carried regular 'sensational' reports.*

Left: This portrait of Wheeler (1890–1976) was taken about the time of the excavations (© National Museum of Wales).

previously unexcavated. An almost complete outline plan of the fortress has been recovered. Parts of the fortress — the amphitheatre, Prysg Field barracks, the fortress baths and the south-western defences — are now on view to the public, and many of the finds from *Isca* are displayed by Amgueddfa Cymru – National Museum Wales in the National Roman Legion Museum. Almost all significant pieces of undeveloped ground within the fortress and its suburbs are now protected as Scheduled Ancient Monuments.

A silver denarius of the emperor Augustus (27 BC–AD 14). The Second Augustan Legion was named after the emperor who had raised or reformed it. A denarius itself represented just over a day's pay for a second-century AD legionary soldier (© National Museum of Wales).

The Legion and its Fortress

In the second century of the Christian era, the empire of Rome comprehended the fairest part of the earth, and the most civilized portion of mankind. The frontiers of that extensive monarchy were guarded by ancient renown and disciplined valour.

Edward Gibbon, *The History of the Decline and Fall of the Roman Empire* (1776–81).

The Second Augustan Legion (*Legio Secunda Augusta*) was one of about thirty Roman legions whose fortresses guarded the frontiers of the empire, from Inchtuthil on the edge of the Scottish Highlands to Bostra in the Arabian desert. Each legion comprised about 5,500 heavily armed infantry, all Roman citizens, and other necessary service personnel.

Legio II Augusta was named after Augustus, the emperor who had raised or reformed it, much as a modern regiment might be called the King's Own, or the Queen's Regiment. Legions usually had both a number and a title. The title was sometimes a nickname in origin, as with *VI Ferrata*, 'The Ironsides' or 'Iron Shod', or sometimes the name of a province in which the legion had served with distinction, such as *IX Hispana*, 'Spanish'. The name could also reflect a battle honour; *XX Valeria Victrix*, for example, probably won its title 'Valorous and Victorious', for its role in the defeat of Queen Boudicca (Boadicea).

From time to time, legions were destroyed in battle or disbanded after a mutiny, and emperors would sometimes raise new legions. Hence, the legionary numbers were not a consecutive series and there were other second legions besides *II Augusta*.

The commanding officer of the legion was a legionary legate. From an aristocratic Roman family of senatorial rank, he held command as part of a

Above: Roman soldiers portrayed on a first-century AD sculptured pillar base from the legionary fortress in Mainz, Germany. The front figure carries the legionary's characteristic rectangular shield (scutum) and short sword (gladius) (Römisch-Germanische Zentralmuseum, Mainz; photo: AKG Images/Erich Lessing).

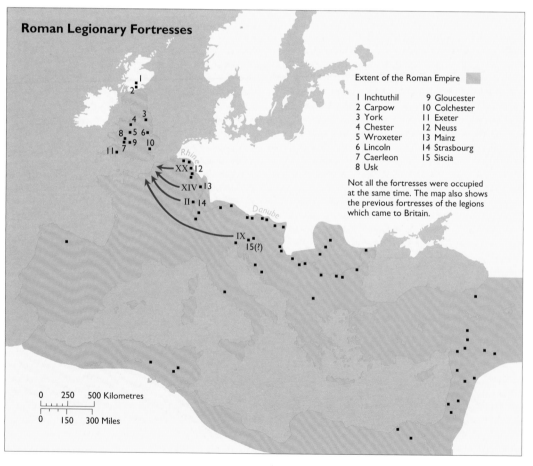

Roman Legionary Fortresses

Extent of the Roman Empire

1	Inchtuthil	9	Gloucester
2	Carpow	10	Colchester
3	York	11	Exeter
4	Chester	12	Neuss
5	Wroxeter	13	Mainz
6	Lincoln	14	Strasbourg
7	Caerleon	15	Siscia
8	Usk		

Not all the fortresses were occupied at the same time. The map also shows the previous fortresses of the legions which came to Britain.

0 250 500 Kilometres

0 150 300 Miles

career as a soldier and administrator. He would have served his military apprenticeship as senior tribune or staff officer in a legion and, if he measured up to the job, he might look forward to being appointed by the emperor to a provincial governorship, and perhaps to the dignity of a consulship in Rome. Below the legate were six tribunes, the senior a young man of similar background to the legate. The others were from more modest families, *equites* ('Roman knights'). They also followed career paths as soldiers and administrators, though in lower grade posts than those reserved for the senatorial aristocracy.

A legion was divided into ten cohorts. The first cohort, at the time Caerleon was founded, consisted of about 800 men in five centuries of double size; each of the remaining cohorts contained 480 men in six centuries, made up of 80 men apiece and commanded by a centurion . Usually promoted from the ranks, centurions were formidable figures, and provided the backbone of the legion. Some of Kipling's unflattering portraits of Victorian sergeant majors in India would have been instantly recognizable to a ranker of *Legio II Augusta*, but in practice the centurion's responsibilities were more equivalent to those of the modern company commander — a major or a senior captain — with full charge of his 80 men.

Far left: This inscription from Caerleon records the restoration of the temple of Diana by the legion's commanding officer, the legionary legate, Titus Flavius Postumius Varus, about AD 250. Like many other commanding officers, he pursued a successful career as a Roman administrator, and during the reign of the emperor Aurelian (AD 270–75) he became prefect of Rome (© National Museum of Wales).

Left: An illustration of a Roman legionary soldier, based upon a reconstruction of the armour and equipment in use during the later first century AD. The Capricorn insignia and legend, LEG II AVG, on his shield show that he belongs to the Second Augustan Legion (Illustration by Geraint Derbyshire).

The Foundation of Isca

When the Romans invaded Britain in AD 43, the emperor Claudius's army comprised four legions and a roughly equal number of non-citizen auxiliary troops. The four legions were *II Augusta*, previously stationed at Strasbourg on the Rhine frontier; two other Rhineland legions, *XX* (later *Valeria Victrix*) from Neuss and *XIV Gemina* from Mainz, and *IX Hispana* from Pannonia in modern Hungary or Slovenia.

II Augusta served with distinction under its commander, Titus Flavius Vespasianus, in south-west England and the Isle of Wight. From about AD 55, the legion was stationed at Exeter, Devon, where

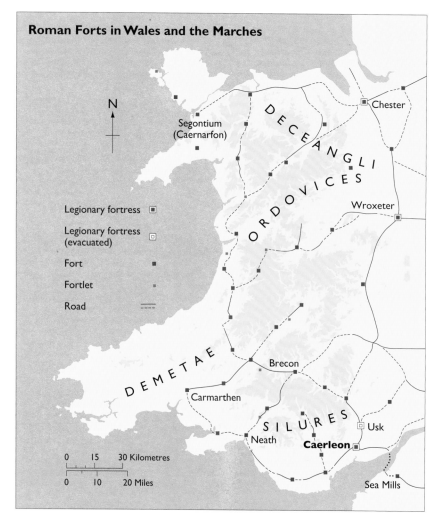

Roman Forts in Wales and the Marches

N

DECEANGLI

ORDOVICES

DEMETAE

SILURES

Chester

Segontium
(Caernarfon)

Wroxeter

Brecon

Carmarthen

Neath

Caerleon

Usk

Sea Mills

Legionary fortress

Legionary fortress
(evacuated)

Fort

Fortlet

Road

| 0 | 15 | 30 Kilometres |
| 0 | 10 | 20 Miles |

A coin of the emperor Vespasian (AD 69–79). He had earlier commanded the Second Legion with distinction during the initial phases of the Roman conquest of southern Britain (© National Museum of Wales).

excavations have revealed parts of an early legionary fortress built in timber, with ranks of barrack blocks and other buildings, including stone baths as large as the Caerleon fortress baths (pp. 20–29). *Legio XX* was probably based at Usk, north of Caerleon, in the same period, but when the number of British legions was reduced to three in AD 66, with the removal of *Legio XIV Gemina*, it took over the latter's old base at Wroxeter in Shropshire.

Vespasian, by then commanding the Roman army against the Jews in Palestine, made a bid for the imperial throne during the civil war that followed the suicide of Nero in AD 68. *II Augusta* played a central role in persuading the other British legions to declare for its old commanding officer and in AD 69 Vespasian became the first emperor of the new Flavian dynasty.

Legio II Augusta may have remained at Exeter or moved to a new fortress at Gloucester in the mid-60s. The new emperor, who had made his reputation as a fighting soldier on the frontiers of the empire in Judaea and Britain, began a new forward policy in the as yet unconquered areas of Britain. The governor of an active military province like Britain would be chosen by the emperor with special regard to the task in hand, and for his particular experience and ability. Vespasian's first governor, Petillius Cerialis (AD 71–74), had the task of settling affairs in northern England, but once this had been done, the next priority was the final pacification of what is now Wales.

Vespasian's choice for this task was Sextus Julius Frontinus (governor AD 74–78), an experienced soldier and in later life a writer of important books on military tactics and on the water supply of Rome (he became director of the organization responsible for the city's water supply). The historian, Tacitus, whose praise was not easily won, thought him 'a truly great man ... he conquered the powerful and warlike tribe of the Silures, overcoming not only a fierce and stubborn enemy, but the difficulties of the terrain'.

The Silures, whose territories included much of south-east Wales, had resisted a series of Roman governors for nearly thirty years, and had inflicted several major defeats on the legions. Frontinus's strategy included moving the Second Legion to a new fortress well inside Silurian territory, to a site where supplies could be brought in by sea. Cerialis had done much the same thing a few years earlier in the north, and the soundness of his choice for *Legio IX's* new fortress is endorsed by the later history of the city of York.

The site of the new legionary fortress was carefully chosen, probably by Frontinus himself. It was a textbook siting for a Roman fort, on a gently elevated plateau or river terrace at a good bridging point of the Usk, and close enough to its mouth to be reached easily by sea-going ships. The new fortress was protected by a broad loop of the river and by a small tributary, the Afon Lwyd. It lay on flat ground, clear of the floodplain, where a suitable gradient for drains and sewers could be created by the engineers. No traces of an earlier camp have been found on the site, despite many years of excavation.

Such a camp might be expected somewhere in the vicinity, but, until the river was bridged and docking facilities were built, the site of the later fortress would have had no overriding advantage. An earlier and much smaller Roman camp may remain undiscovered somewhere in the Caerleon area, but it will have been sited for tactical rather than for strategic reasons, and need not have been on the site of the later *Isca*.

The Second Legion and the Occupation of Caerleon

The legion contained over 5,000 men but, save in the initial campaign against the Silures, the whole force would rarely have fought together as a single unit. Detachments or vexillations, so known from their *vexillum* or banner, were

An aerial view of the fortress of Isca *(Caerleon) from the south, showing the characteristic playing-card shape of the defences (highlighted with a red line). The amphitheatre lay outside the defensive line. The Roman bridge over the Usk stood on the bend of the river, to the right of the present crossing. (RCAHMW: Crown Copyright).*

Right: Detachments from Legio II Augusta *served in parts of the Roman empire far from Caerleon. The death of a soldier on campaign in Germany is recorded on a tombstone erected by Tadia Exuperata, a resident of one of the civilian settlements around Isca. 'To the spirits of the departed: Tadia Vallaunius lived 65 years and Tadius Exuper(a)tus, her son, lived 37 years, having died on the German expedition...' (© National Museum of Wales).*

A bronze head (above) of the emperor Hadrian (AD 117–38) found in the river Thames in 1834 (Courtesy of the Trustees of the British Museum). Hadrian began his frontier wall across northern Britain in AD 122 (right), where stonemasons from at least seven of the ten cohorts of Legio II Augusta *are known to have been engaged in work (English Heritage). This inscription (centre right) from milecastle 38, on the central sector of Hadrian's Wall, records the legion at work there under the governor Aulus Platorius Nepos in AD 122–26 (Museum of Antiquities of the University and Society of Antiquaries of Newcastle-upon-Tyne).*

detached for campaigns in northern Britain or on one of the other frontiers of the empire. There are numerous records of such vexillations of *II Augusta*; a tombstone from Caerleon was set up by a lady to her mother and to her brother, Tadius Exuperatus, who died 'on the German expedition'. With Siluria peaceful, an increasing number of troops could have been drafted away. Barracks would be left empty and increasingly *Isca* became a regimental base depot rather than an active military garrison.

When the emperor Hadrian began his great frontier wall across northern Britain in AD 122, much of the Roman army in Britain was drafted to this area. Inscriptions from Hadrian's Wall record the efforts of the many craftsmen, including stonemasons, from seven out of ten cohorts of *II Augusta* who were at work there. The absence of the other three from the surviving inscriptions may be due to chance. When the Roman frontier was advanced into southern Scotland under Antoninus Pius twenty years later, a fresh series of inscriptions show that much of the legion was again on the northern frontier.

It was once thought that with the legion away, *Isca* lay empty at this time, but archaeological evidence shows that occupation continued, at least in some parts of the fortress. Our evidence is too slight to reconstruct what must have been complicated troop movements, but at the Prysg Field barracks it would seem that some of them were occupied, perhaps one

The church of St Cadoc stands over part of the principia — *the headquarters building — at the centre of the fortress. The great hall — the* basilica — *of the headquarters was probably raised in stone in the late first century.*

per cohort. It may have been that each cohort needed to maintain a presence at the base depot for recruits, and for soldiers rejoining their unit or waiting to be reassigned. Indeed, base depots can be busy places in wartime, even if the unit is on active service elsewhere.

The murder of the emperor Commodus in AD 192 ended the Antonine age — the 'high summer' of the Roman empire. In the ensuing scramble for power, Septimius Severus eventually emerged as the victor. In the process, at Lyons, he had bloodily defeated the British legions, including *II Augusta*, who had supported the British contender for power, Clodius Albinus. The withdrawal of the army from Britain opened the gates to Caledonian invaders, and the northern frontier was overrun. It took a series of hard fought campaigns in the north and in Scotland, some led by the emperor in person, before stability was restored.

A fine inscription dug up in the churchyard at Caerleon records the restoration of the headquarters building under Severus and his sons, Caracalla and Geta, sometime before the latter was murdered by his brother in AD 211. On this, and on one of the two inscriptions set up by a legionary prefect for the health and safety of the imperial family, Geta's name has been erased by order of his brother. Geta had become what George Orwell called an 'unperson'.

The legionary headquarters was evidently still at Caerleon in the early part of Severus's reign, when the northern frontier was gradually being restored. At this time, *II Augusta* was no doubt being brought back to full strength after its heavy losses at Lyons, and the subsequent very thorough purge of officers loyal to Clodius Albinus. By AD 208 Severus was ready to take the offensive in Scotland and *II Augusta* would have marched north. During these campaign years, part of the legion was stationed in a new legionary base at Carpow on the Tay. Possibly it was intended to transfer the legion there permanently,

*This fine inscription, cut on five blocks of stone (only one survives), was dug up about 1850 in St Cadoc's churchyard. It records the reconstruction of the legionary headquarters building under the emperor Septimius Severus (AD 193–211) and his sons, Caracalla and Geta. The building had fallen into decay through age (*vetustate corruptum*) and was restored about AD 198–209. Geta's name was erased after his murder by Caracalla in AD 211 (© National Museum of Wales).*

IMPERATORES ANTONINVS VETVSTATE / CAESARESLSEPTI AVGETPSEPTIMIVS CORRVPTVM / MIVS SEVERVS PIVS GETA NOBILISSIMVS / PERTINAX AVG·ET CAESAR / · M·AVRELIVS RESTITVERVNT

Above: Caracalla, whose official name was Antoninus, granted the Second Legion the title Antoniniana (Caracalla's Own), and this appears with the legionary stamp (LEG II AUG ANTO) on roof tiles from the fortress (© National Museum of Wales).

Right: A statue base from Caerwent with an inscription dedicated to Tiberius Claudius Paulinus, a commanding officer of the Second Legion around AD 214–17. Paulinus may have become a patron of the Roman town.

An inscription recording the complete reconstruction of the seventh cohort's barracks during the reigns of the emperors Valerian and Gallienus around AD 253–58 (© National Museum of Wales).

and a start may well have been made on dismantling *Isca*. In AD 211–12, however, Caracalla made peace, and soon after this *Isca* was extensively renovated.

The south-west gate, near the amphitheatre, may have been restored under Caracalla, judging by an inscription found near it. In addition, the amphitheatre was remodelled and barrack blocks were repaired and reroofed. The legionary tile kilns were busy producing large quantities of roofing tiles, stamped LEG II AUG ANTO, with the title *Antoniniana* — 'Caracalla's Own' — granted to the legion by the emperor. About AD 214–17, during a period at *Isca*, the legionary legate, Tiberius Claudius Paulinus, may have become patron of the town of *Venta Silurum* (Caerwent). Later in his career he was able to obtain some substantial official favour for the town — possibly a tax exemption — and was honoured by the grateful local authority with a statue, the inscribed base of which survives.

The campaigns of Severus maintained stability in Britain for two generations, and the army went about the routine business of peace-time soldiering. At Caerleon, the fortress baths were operating down to AD 230 or 240 and some of the Prysg Field barracks were occupied until the same date. In AD 234, and again in 244, we have evidence that the *primus pilus* or senior centurion of *Legio II Augusta*, who had charge of the legionary eagle standard, dedicated an altar to the eagle of the legion on its official birthday (23 September). The dedication and ceremonial parade were attended by the units of the legion then at Caerleon, whose main body was evidently still based there. However, the murders of the emperors Severus Alexander in AD 235 and Gordian III in 244 began a period of political anarchy. By the time the next such ceremony was due, the core of the legion may have been called away to fight for one of the numerous ephemeral emperors of the third century.

This was not the end of *Isca*. Most of it lay empty, though the fortress baths and perhaps other main buildings seem to have been in the hands of a care and maintenance squad. It may well have been that the number of soldiers still there did not justify such extensive facilities and one of the smaller extramural baths could have sufficed. Nonetheless, it was still the legionary base depot and in AD 253–58 the seventh cohort was posted back there after a spell on duty elsewhere. Their barracks needed to be totally rebuilt, as demonstrated by an inscription.

Fragments of a recently discovered inscription record further building activity under Aurelian in AD 274–75, perhaps the restoration of other barracks.

As well as changes at Caerleon itself, the legions of the late empire were very different from those of Trajan or Hadrian. The latter were formidable in battle, but too large and immobile for rapid deployment to a threatened frontier, particularly after they had put down roots in a fortress like

Caerleon, where soldiers were recruited from local families. In practice, a detachment of perhaps two cohorts (1,000 men) was more useful. Such a vexillation might be detached from its parent unit for a long period, or might never return to its home province. A third-century silvered-bronze disc first recorded in Italy shows vexillations of two British legions, *II Augusta* and the Chester legion, *XX Valeria Victrix*, who were probably serving on the Rhine or Danube frontier. The disc depicts the legions with their standards and their legionary emblems, the Capricorn and the Boar, and demonstrates how legionary uniforms and weapons had changed.

The end seems to have come for *Isca* when the usurper, Carausius (AD 287–93), who had seized power in Britain, expected invasion from the Continent by the legitimate emperors Diocletian and Constantius. Some time between

Left: The tombstone of a centurion of the Second Augustan Legion, Vivius Marcianus, who was on detachment in London when he died in the third century (By permission of the Museum of London).

Above: This third-century silvered-bronze disc shows units, or vexillations, of two British legions — II Augusta and XX Valeria Victrix — brigaded together for service on the Rhine or Danube. The removal of such units for service elsewhere explains why parts of the fortress fell into disuse during the third century (By courtesy of the Bibliothèque Nationale de France, Paris).

A section of the fourth-century stone walls surrounding the Roman town at Caerwent. It was one of a series of late Roman defended sites around the western and southern coastlines of Britain.

Above: A coin of the usurper Carausius (AD 287–93) during whose reign the fortress of Isca may have been finally given up by the Roman army. The Second Legion was needed to defend the south coast against invasion by legitimate emperors (© National Museum of Wales).

AD 287 and 296 Carausius, or his murderer and successor, Allectus (AD 293–96), demolished the main buildings of the fortress, perhaps so that the materials could be re-used in new defences elsewhere. There were threats from sea-borne raiders along the south-east coast, and a late Roman army and civil service list records the presence of the Second Augustan Legion at one of Carausius's new ' Saxon shore' forts at Richborough in Kent. As a 'legion', however, it would have been unrecognizable to a soldier who had served at Caerleon in the time of Trajan or Hadrian. By the fourth century, the front line troops were no longer the legions and auxiliaries but the mobile field armies in attendance on the emperor, which could be moved rapidly to any threatened area. As a consequence, the old legions declined in status and size; they were regarded as second-class troops, probably with establishment sizes reduced from 5,500 to around 1,000 men.

The presence of early fourth-century coins suggests that occupation continued at Caerleon after Carausius, though whether this was military is unclear. There were fourth-century military defences along the south Wales coastal plain at Caerwent and Cardiff, and the key river crossing at Caerleon linking the two would still have been important. Roman coins at Caerleon are not uncommon down to the time of the usurper, Magnentius (AD 350–53), who removed troops from Britain to fight against the legitimate emperor. In this final period, the courtyard of the baths was used as a cattle pen, and low-quality dwellings or stalls were put up in parts of its surrounding portico. The bare shell of the fortress baths was to survive through to medieval times, but by this time the history of *Isca* was long over and that of Caerleon had begun.

The Layout of the Fortress

The fortress covered an area of some 50 acres (20.5ha), and was shaped rather like a playing card. The angles of the great sweeping defences were rounded for greater stability and a better field of fire. There were four gates, one in the centre of each side, though nothing of these now remains above ground.

The Defences

When first built, about AD 75, the defences were of turf, clay and timber. Later, the bank was fronted with a wall of mortared masonry, and its timber gates replaced in stone.

Legionaries were skilled in the art of building turf and clay ramparts. Sometimes a foundation of oak logs was laid under the bank to provide a firm foundation. Indeed, strapping of this kind was found under part of the rampart in Prysg Field, though it seems only in one small area. Turves were cut to a standard regulation size for ease of carrying and laying, and were used with clay, from the digging of the ditch, to form a rampart with a near-vertical front face some 18 feet (5.5m) broad

A section of the clay and turf fortress rampart, seen during an excavation along the south-western defences. The stone walls and towers were built on to the front of the earlier rampart (Photograph by Howard Mason).

Every Roman legion contained skilled architects, surveyors and builders. This relief from Trajan's Column, erected in Rome in the early first century AD, shows legionaries working on both timber and masonry structures.

Above: An artist's reconstruction of the defences in the north-western corner of the fortress, as they may have appeared in the late first century. The defences and barracks are shown in timber, but there is no certain evidence for the towers (Illustration by John Banbury, 1988, after Howard Mason).

Right: All of the principal buildings were roofed with tiles. The gable ends often carried ornaments (antefixa), *with devices such as this gorgon's head intended to avert evil and to protect those within (© National Museum of Wales).*

and perhaps 8 to 10 feet (2.5 to 3m) high. The bank would have been topped with a timber palisade or fighting top and a rampart walkway. It was perhaps reinforced, like the later stone defences, with towers set at intervals. No certain evidence of such timber towers has been found, perhaps because all traces were destroyed when the replacement stone defences were built. But towers would certainly have increased the potential field of fire, particularly into the ditch bottom, where attackers might otherwise shelter out of reach of missiles from the rampart.

Inside the bank, a perimeter road — the *via sagularis* ('cloak street') — gave troops rapid

access to the rampart in case of attack. In front of the bank was the fortress ditch, now entirely silted up, though cross-sections have been cut archaeologically at a number of points. The ditch was around 8 or 9 feet (2.5 or 2.7m) deep and about 26 feet (8m) wide. The profile was V-shaped where it cut through the clay, but was flatter where it met the sandstone bedrock. With its sloping sides of slippery clay, and its bottom gradually silted with wet, black mud, it would have presented a formidable obstacle.

The Internal Layout

Within the defences, the buildings were laid out to a pattern standard in legionary fortresses. With rare exceptions, notably the fortress baths, the commanding officer's house and the *fabrica* (a large workshop complex), they were first constructed of timber. Before modern techniques of 'open area' excavation were in use, archaeologists usually concentrated on the later stone buildings, exploring the earlier timber phase only in narrow cuttings. Our knowledge of the first-century fortress is therefore very limited, though where it has been tested its layout is followed in precise detail by the later stone-built arrangement. Indeed, the overall plan of *Isca* probably originated with the initial foundation, with individual timber buildings replaced in stone when the need arose, or when building capacity became available.

Far left: 'To the Emperor Caesar Nerva Trajan Augustus, conqueror of Germany, son of the deified Nerva…'. This inscription of Tuscan marble records the rebuilding in stone of one of the major buildings or gates of the fortress in AD 100 (© National Museum of Wales).

Left: A stone screen that probably formed part of one of the administrative buildings in the fortress. A portion of the painted decoration has been reconstructed in colours similar to those that may have been used (© National Museum of Wales).

In the centre of the fortress (in the area under the present church) stood the *principia* or headquarters, where the legionary eagle and standards were kept and a statue of the reigning emperor displayed. A massive four-way triumphal arch provided an imposing approach to the headquarters building, while the official residence of the legionary legate lay to the east of the *principia*. The main street of the fortress (*via principalis*) ran in front of the headquarters, and opposite was a row of officers' houses. The *via principalis* divided the fortress into two almost equal halves. The front half (*praetentura*) held the fortress baths and probably the hospital. The rear (*retentura*) contained the workshops for the legionary craftsmen — including masons, carpenters, blacksmiths, tanners, metalworkers in lead and bronze, shoemakers (more than 5,000 pairs of military boots would have needed constant repair), and others. Other areas within the defences would have held the granaries, together with a range of other buildings including a prison.

The front and rear ranges of the fortress, and areas flanking the *principia*, held the ranges of long, narrow barrack blocks: one for each century, therefore six for each of the ten cohorts, and so sixty in total (though at the time Caerleon was founded the first cohort of each legion comprised five double centuries and therefore needed additional barracks: p. 7). This layout was repeated, with some variation, at fortresses throughout the empire, so that legionaries newly posted to *II Augusta* from north Africa or the Danube would have found their way around *Isca* without undue difficulty.

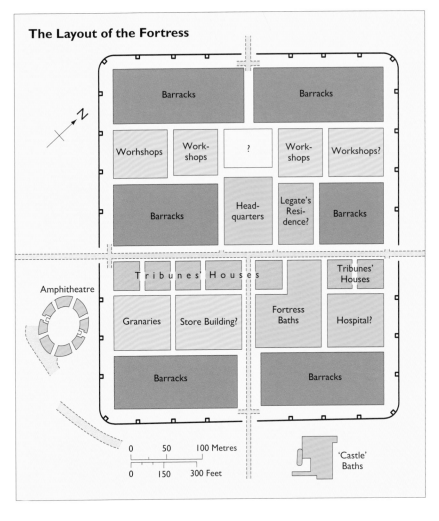

The Layout of the Fortress

Barracks · Barracks · Worhshops · Work-shops · ? · Work-shops · Workshops? · Barracks · Head-quarters · Legate's Resi-dence? · Barracks · Tribunes' Houses · Tribunes' Houses · Amphitheatre · Granaries · Store Building? · Fortress Baths · Hospital? · Barracks · Barracks

0 50 100 Metres
0 150 300 Feet

'Castle' Baths

A Tour of Roman Isca

The Roman monuments of Caerleon are all within a few minutes walk in and around the pleasant small town. Visitors arriving at the fortress baths in the centre of the town may then walk some 80 yards (73m) down the main street to the National Roman Legion Museum by the church. The museum contains an extensive display of Roman artefacts recovered from the legionary fortress and its environs. There is also a full-scale reconstruction of part of a Roman barrack block. From the museum, a quiet road (locally known as Broadway) runs along the line of the Roman *via principalis* and leads to the amphitheatre. Footpaths branch off to the right (north-west) for the Prysg Field barracks, and to the left (south-east) for the fortress defences.

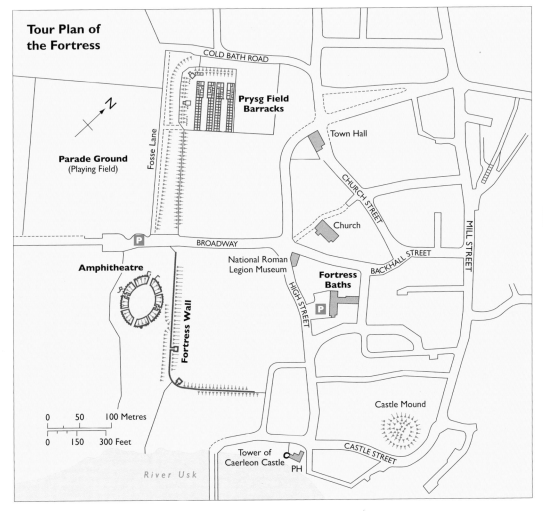

Tour Plan of the Fortress

COLD BATH ROAD

Prysg Field Barracks

Fosse Lane

Parade Ground (Playing Field)

Town Hall

CHURCH STREET

Church

BROADWAY

MILL STREET

BACKHALL STREET

Amphitheatre

National Roman Legion Museum

Fortress Baths

HIGH STREET

Fortress Wall

Castle Mound

0   50   100 Metres
0   150   300 Feet

CASTLE STREET

Tower of Caerleon Castle

PH

River Usk

Above: The Capricorn insignia of the Second Augustan Legion, from a silver denarius of the emperor Vespasian (© National Museum of Wales).

Opposite: The superb collection of 88 engraved gemstones discovered during the 1979 excavation of the fortress baths drain. They range in date from the first to the early third centuries AD (© National Museum of Wales).

The Fortress Baths

At the end of the car park, under a modern cover building, are parts of the legionary fortress baths, so named to distinguish them from other bath buildings outside the fortress defences. Standing in the car park, you may care to pause and consider the baths in their original setting.

At this point, High Street is on the line of the *via praetoria*, one of the main roads of the fortress, which led up from the bridge across the Usk to the headquarters building in the centre. In Roman times, the area of the car park would have been a large colonnaded courtyard (*palaestra*) for open-air games and exercise. At its far end, under the front of the cover building, was a long narrow open-air swimming pool or *natatio*, with an apsidal fountain house at one end. Behind this was the bath building proper, comprising a succession of three lofty, vaulted halls. On the left, within the cover building, the first of these halls was the cold bath hall or *frigidarium*. This led on to the right (under the modern gardens and houses) to the warm bath suite or *tepidarium* and the hot baths or *caldarium*. To the left of the cover building (below more modern gardens and houses) was a great aisled exercise hall or *basilica*.

Our knowledge of the overall plan and development of the baths is based on a series of archaeological excavations conducted at various times between 1964 and 1981. On entering the cover building, it is important to appreciate that only two areas of the baths provide the focus of the visible remains; the swimming pool (*natatio*) and the cold bath suite (*frigidarium*). A glance at the accompanying plans, together with the illuminating site graphics, should enable you to place these remains in context.

The Scale of the Bath Building

Inside the modern cover building, you will begin to appreciate the impressive scale of the baths structure. The site exhibition, which includes reconstructions, a detailed architectural model of the building and spoken commentaries, may be consulted independently of this guidebook.

The construction of the baths began around AD 75–77, more or less at the same time that the fortress was established. The massive construction of stone and concrete would have towered over the remainder of the fortress, which at this time was built almost entirely of timber. Concrete and the size of the vaulted spans it made possible were still fairly novel at the time. There was room for architects and engineers to experiment, and the superstructure and vaults of the fortress baths may have resembled the surviving *frigidarium* of the Cluny baths in Paris. The building may indeed have anticipated the design of the great imperial baths of Rome itself, notably in the symmetrical planning and vault design.

In scale, and to some extent in plan, the fortress baths can be compared with a medieval cathedral, with its aisled *basilica* matching the nave, and the three halls of the bath suite the chancel. The overall length of some 360 feet (110m) equals, for example, that of Wells Cathedral. In turn, the vaulted ceiling of the bath suite would have been at roughly the height of the roof vault in a later cathedral.

Various archaeological excavations conducted between 1964 and 1981 exposed the remains of the fortress baths. This picture shows work underway on the cold bath hall (frigidarium) in 1979 (© National Museum of Wales).

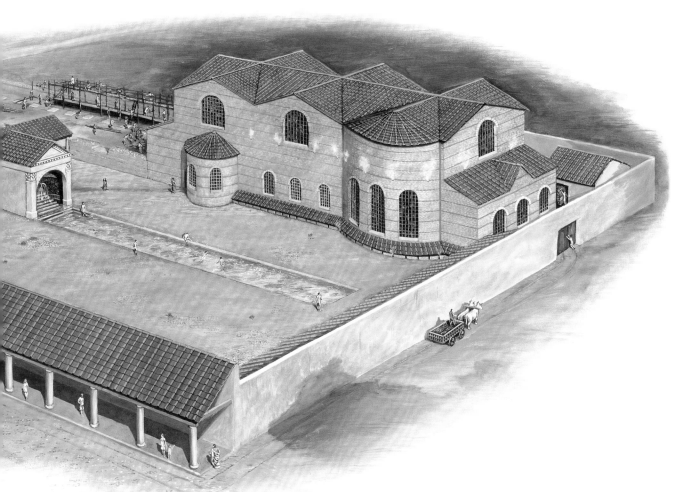

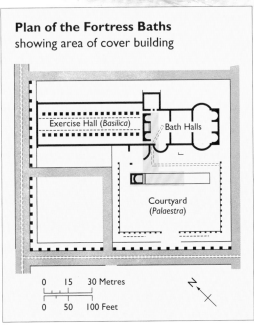

Plan of the Fortress Baths
showing area of cover building

Exercise Hall (*Basilica*)

Bath Halls

Courtyard
(*Palaestra*)

| 0 | 15 | 30 Metres |
| 0 | 50 | 100 Feet |

Above: An artist's impression of the fortress baths complex as it may have appeared about AD 80, with the great exercise hall (basilica) shown under construction. The open-air swimming pool (natatio) with its fountain house, fronts a courtyard which now lies beneath the modern car park. The roadway in front of the colonnade runs below the busy modern High Street (Illustration by Paul Jenkins, 1987; © National Museum of Wales).

Left: The Cluny baths in Paris survive as one of the city's major museums. The huge cold hall gives an impression of the appearance and scale of that at Caerleon (David Robinson).

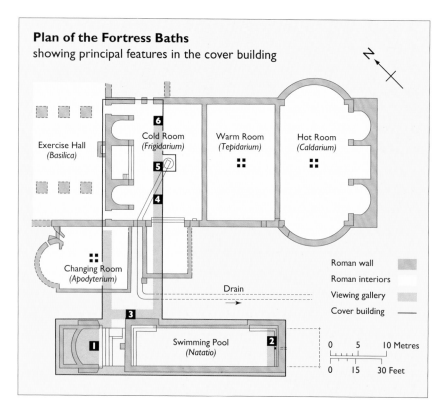

Plan of the Fortress Baths
showing principal features in the cover building

Exercise Hall
(Basilica)

6
Cold Room
(Frigidarium)

Warm Room
(Tepidarium)

Hot Room
(Caldarium)

5

4

Changing Room
(Apodyterium)

Drain

3

1

Swimming Pool
(Natatio)

2

Roman wall

Roman interiors

Viewing gallery

Cover building

0   5   10 Metres

0   15   30 Feet

The Swimming Pool (Natatio)

The first structure you now encounter within the cover building was originally a swimming pool, situated in the open air. It stood at the end of the courtyard between the baths and the main street, with the principal wall of the bath building proper rising behind it. Supplied with a continuous flow of water through lead pipes, the pool held some 80,250 gallons (365,000 l) and was 135 feet (41 m) long, with a larger surface area than the Great Bath at *Aquae Sulis*, Bath.

At one end (under the platform where you now enter) [1] was a half-round fountain house or *nymphaeum*, with the foundation of its apse still visible. Smaller examples from Pompeii and elsewhere suggest that this would have been richly decorated. Part of a stone dolphin from a sculpture group survives and is on display, and fragments of wall plaster found during excavation show that the apse was painted with a colourful aquatic or garden scene. Water, from a tank behind the apse, would have gushed from the mouth of the dolphin. The sculpture group of which it formed part probably

Right: An artist's impression of the fountain house, at one end of the swimming bath, as it may have appeared when first constructed (Illustration by John Banbury, 1988, after J. D. Zienkiewicz, 1986).

Below: A carved-stone dolphin head which probably formed part of a sculpture group within the apse of the fountain house.

included figures of Venus and a cupid. In front, the water cascaded down a flight of steps clad in broad slabs of Purbeck marble, parts of which remain in place. These steps did not give access to the pool. Later, steps for bathers were provided at one side.

From the shallow end, some 4 feet (1.2m) deep, the water shelved to about 5 feet (1.6m) at the deep end. The walls of the *natatio* were built of flanged roofing tiles set in mortar, with a waterproof cement rendering on the face. Originally, the floor was of concrete mixed with crushed brick (the present gravel finish is modern).

About AD 87–95, the baths were refurbished and the floor and sides of the pool were lined with flagstones, though in turn these were removed in a later phase; only traces of their impressions in the mortar bed remain. About forty years later, the pool was radically altered. The fountain house appears to have been prone to subsidence, and was now demolished, though the sculpture group was perhaps

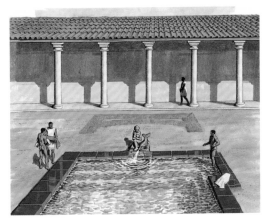

set up elsewhere. The pool itself was shortened when two blocking walls were inserted across it and the area behind them filled-in. The length of the *natatio* was thus reduced from 135 feet (41m) to some 84 feet (25.5m).

The new shorter pool was lined with sandstone slabs; these too were later removed. The north-west

Above: A view along the length of the open-air swimming bath, seen from the fountain house. The blocking wall in the foreground formed part of the mid-second-century alterations to the baths; the fountain house was taken down and the pool shortened.

Left: An artist's impression of the shortened swimming bath (natatio) of the mid-second century. The fountain house apse to the rear has been demolished (Illustration by John Banbury, 1988, after J. D. Zienkiewicz, 1986).

In the foreground of this view, the crown of the main bathhouse drain is seen turning at what was once the edge of a courtyard. To the top left, the small brick pillars survive from an underfloor heating system beneath a changing room. To the top right, the curved edge and paved floor mark the position of a cold plunge bath.

blocking wall, of stone and red tile with a strengthening buttress behind it, can be seen (near the entrance of the cover building), with steps for bathers in front of it. The fill behind has been removed, and this enables us to see the original length of the pool, along with the foundation of the fountain house.

At the opposite end of the pool [2] the outer face of the other later blocking wall is visible. Again, there are steps in front, and it still has its lead outlet pipe.

It was perhaps at the time of Septimius Severus's campaigns in Scotland (AD 208–11) that the stone slabs lining the pool were removed. Their removal may have been linked to a planned abandonment of the fortress at this time (pp. 11–12). Soon after this, however, the pool was given a new cement lining and, although less grand, it continued in use until about AD 240.

The Heated Changing Room (Apodyterium)

The coarse grey gravel around the swimming pool, though modern, shows the area of the open-air exercise yard (*palaestra*) in which it stood. If you now turn from the *natatio*, towards the other long axis of the cover building, beyond the coarse gravel, we may next consider the remains of the bath building itself [3].

The remains at this end (nearest the *natatio*) include a heated changing room (*apodyterium*) and a cold plunge bath. The changing room can be seen at basement level to the left, and is distinguished by the rows of small, square brick pillars of its hypocaust or

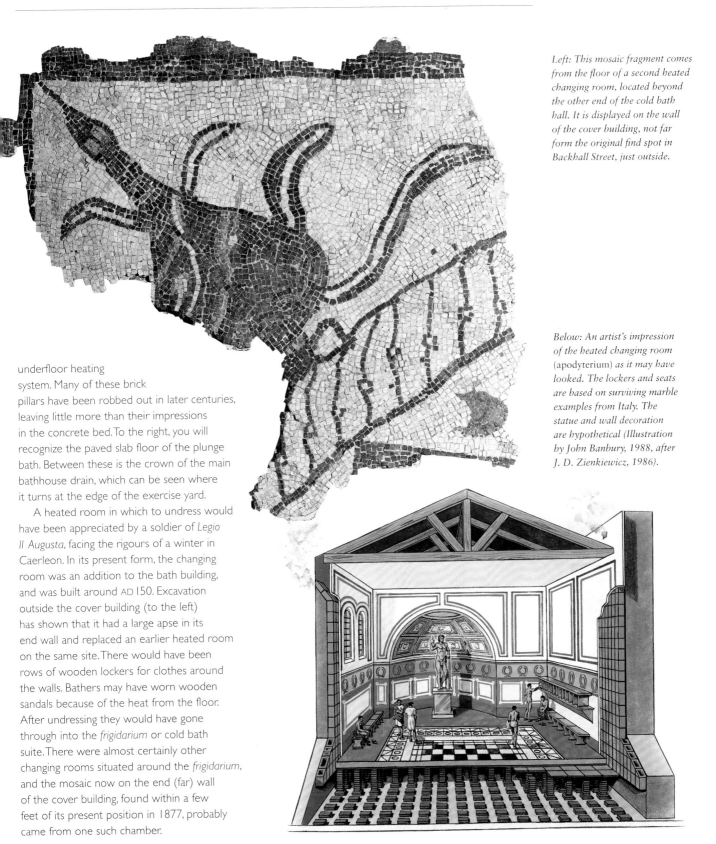

Left: This mosaic fragment comes from the floor of a second heated changing room, located beyond the other end of the cold bath hall. It is displayed on the wall of the cover building, not far form the original find spot in Backhall Street, just outside.

Below: An artist's impression of the heated changing room (apodyterium) as it may have looked. The lockers and seats are based on surviving marble examples from Italy. The statue and wall decoration are hypothetical (Illustration by John Banbury, 1988, after J. D. Zienkiewicz, 1986).

underfloor heating system. Many of these brick pillars have been robbed out in later centuries, leaving little more than their impressions in the concrete bed. To the right, you will recognize the paved slab floor of the plunge bath. Between these is the crown of the main bathhouse drain, which can be seen where it turns at the edge of the exercise yard.

A heated room in which to undress would have been appreciated by a soldier of *Legio II Augusta*, facing the rigours of a winter in Caerleon. In its present form, the changing room was an addition to the bath building, and was built around AD 150. Excavation outside the cover building (to the left) has shown that it had a large apse in its end wall and replaced an earlier heated room on the same site. There would have been rows of wooden lockers for clothes around the walls. Bathers may have worn wooden sandals because of the heat from the floor. After undressing they would have gone through into the *frigidarium* or cold bath suite. There were almost certainly other changing rooms situated around the *frigidarium*, and the mosaic now on the end (far) wall of the cover building, found within a few feet of its present position in 1877, probably came from one such chamber.

*Opposite: The triple recesses at
the end of the cold bath hall
originally housed a central cold
plunge bath, flanked by a pair
of basins used for splash bathing.
The arrangement can be seen
in the drawing to the right.*

*This fragment of a round basin
(labrum) was found at the
'Castle' baths outside the fortress
walls in 1849. It is carved from
Purbeck marble and is decorated
with a gorgon's head. Similar
basins were located in recesses
within the original cold hall
building (© National Museum
of Wales).*

The Cold Bath Hall (Frigidarium)

The thick wall beyond the heated changing room (marked by a hanging screen of translucent material) was initially the main external wall of the bath building, before the addition of the later changing room. At this end [**4**], the remains we see are those of part of the *frigidarium*, or cold bath hall. However, only half of this can now be seen. It extends beyond the cover building, where — below the modern gardens and houses — there are the remains of the warm and hot halls. The entire bath building thus continued on to the right, and in fact was six times the length of the visible remains.

The end wall of the cold hall was a massive block of solid masonry, taking some of the weight and thrust of the concrete vaults above. In this wall, at ground level, were triple recesses, comprising a central rectangular bath flanked by semi-circular recesses.

In front of the triple recesses, you will notice a row of regularly spaced, deep, ragged pits. These show the position of large piers, built of blocks of dressed masonry, which were robbed out in medieval times. The hanging screens in the picture opposite show the scale of these piers, and hint at what their decoration may have been like, with fluted pilasters and classical decoration above. The positions of the adjacent windows are also indicated. There was a similar arrangement at the opposite end of the bath suite, forming the end wall of the hot bath hall (*caldarium*). When first built, the two apsidal alcoves housed a pair of circular basins on high pedestals. The bathers would have used the basins to splash down. Part of a similar basin (*labrum*) in Purbeck marble from another Caerleon bathhouse, decorated with a gorgon's head, illustrates the size and shape of these features, and is on exhibition here. Later, the alcoves were turned into additional cold pools. The plaster linings and half-round angle mouldings of these pools survive remarkably intact.

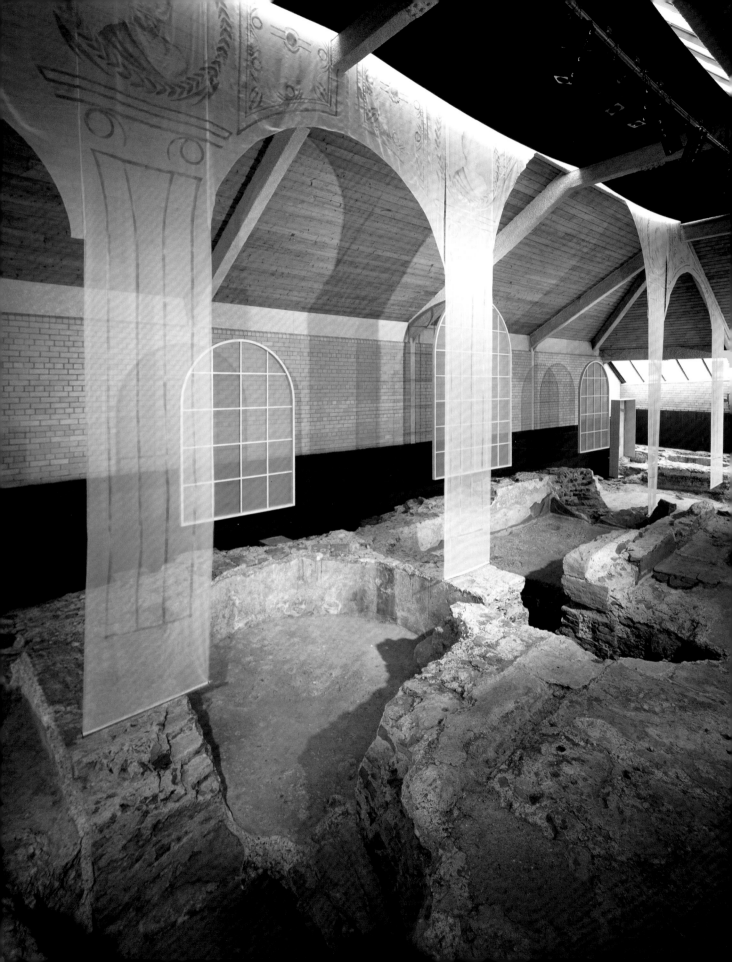

Water splashed across the floor of the cold bath hall passed into the main drain through a perforated cover like this one discovered during the nineteenth-century excavations at the 'Castle' baths (© National Museum of Wales).

The rectangular basin between them still has part of its lining of sandstone slabs.

In front of these recesses, the bath hall had a floor of large rectangular stone flags, parts of which remain. Here, bathers would have stood after a visit to the *caldarium*, and may have splashed themselves down. The floor was given a slight downwards slope towards its centre, where there would have been a circular perforated cover over a drain. The drain carried away all the splashed water, and any overflow from the pools in the baths. The position of this drain opening may be seen in a recess (on the opposite side of the walkway) in the right-hand wall of the cover building [5]. The circular cover has gone, but one stone of its surround, cut to a curve, remains.

A similar drain cover, known from one of the other Caerleon bathhouses, is on display and provides an indication of the design. Below the drain hole itself, a light shows the underlying brick-built *frigidarium* drain.

At the end of the *frigidarium*, a double doorway led through to a second heated chamber [6]. This now lies under Backhall Street to the rear of the cover building. Part of the first-century mosaic pavement from this chamber, found under the street in 1877, has been placed on the end wall. The surviving part shows the end of a Bacchic wand or *thyrsus*, originally borne by devotees of the god Bacchus or Dionysus. In the complete pavement two such wands were probably crossed over a large circular device, possibly a shield.

An artist's impression of Second Legion soldiers enjoying a cold shower at the baths (Illustration by John Banbury).

Roman Bathing: The Legionaries Relax

For the Romans, a bath building was not simply a public bathhouse. It combined the amenities of a modern leisure centre with something of the ambience of a gentlemen's club. Here one could play ball games or gamble, meet one's friends, visit a masseur, buy a pasty, a mutton chop or a roast duck. At *Isca*, wine and beer were also probably served in the fortress baths. In Rome, the major bath buildings included art galleries, as well as Greek and Latin libraries, and could also cater for less elevated tastes.

Women and small children also used the Caerleon baths, as is shown by the numerous hair pins and items of jewellery from the main drain of the fortress baths, along with a number of milk teeth. In some towns, local by-laws decreed that ladies should use the baths in the morning, men in the afternoon. Several emperors found it necessary to forbid mixed bathing, which suggests that it did take place, though perhaps not among respectable women. The baths also served like a modern sports centre or gymnasium, with a swimming bath, a *palaestra* or courtyard for open-air games, and a large aisled hall for indoor exercise.

The End of the Bath Building

As we have seen, the fortress baths appear to have been maintained for use by the legion until AD 230–40. The floors within the building seem generally to have been kept free of rubbish until about AD 270. After that time all hope of reopening the baths was apparently given up and, about AD 290–300, the buildings were stripped of all reusable materials. This enormous structure did, however, survive as a shell until the twelfth or thirteenth century.

In post-Roman times, when the roof and vaults of the baths remained intact, it seems the building became the haunt of barn owls, which roost in derelict roofed structures. This has been deduced from an examination of rodent remains from the excavations, thought to be from the pellets regurgitated by owls.

We should not be surprised that such a formidable construction could survive for so long. Indeed, the Cluny baths in Paris still stand with the *frigidarium* vault intact as part of one of the major museums of the city. Perhaps all that prevented the fortress baths from surviving to our own day in a similar condition was a shortage of building stone, which led the builders of Caerleon Castle or one of the medieval monastic houses of the area to pillage the baths to meet their needs.

A second- or third-century cornelian gemstone engraved with the goddess Roma, recovered from the filling of a large drain beneath the cold hall of the fortress baths (© National Museum of Wales).

A soldier of *Legio II Augusta* coming to the baths would strip, place his clothes in a locker under the care of one of the bathhouse slaves, and pass through into the *frigidarium* or cold bath suite. After a cold dip, he would anoint his body with oils from a glass bath flask, a number of which have been found here during excavation. The legionary would then visit the warm and hot bath suites in turn. Heat from wood-burning furnaces, stoked by soldiers on baths duty, passed through hypocausts, where rows of brick piers supported a raised floor to give underfloor heating. Additional warmth was transmitted through ceramic heating ducts in the walls. Lead or bronze boiler tanks over the furnaces provided hot water.

The oil and sweat would be scraped from the body with a metal scraper or strigil. One bather was unlucky enough to lose one of a set of expensive strigils, richly inlaid with silver, gold and brass, and decorated with the twelve labours of Hercules, which eventually found its way into the bathhouse drain where it was recovered on excavation.

Bathers often wore their rings and other jewellery in the baths (pilfering from lockers was not unknown), and the heat and damp sometimes loosened gemstones from rings, or even the ring itself from the bather's finger. Amongst a host of small objects swept into the bathhouse drain was a superb collection of 88 engraved gemstones of amethyst, cornelian, jasper and other stones. Other small objects recovered from the drain help to fill out our picture of life in the baths: counters for gaming, bone hair pins, together with animal and bird bones and an olive stone from the snacks sold to bathers.

After his hot bath, the legionary would return through the warm and cold rooms, take a final cold dip, and perhaps visit the latrine. He would then dress and return to the baths *basilica* or to the courtyard to watch the ball players, or simply to talk with friends.

Above: Gaming counters and dice found at the fortress baths provide vivid insights into the pastimes enjoyed there. The cup and gaming board shown here are modern reconstructions (© National Museum of Wales).

Left: A glass flask that held oil to anoint a bather's body, and a copper strigil — inlaid with silver and gold — used to scrape away oil and sweat after bathing. They were found in the fortress baths (© National Museum of Wales).

The Amphitheatre

The road from the National Roman Legion Museum and church to the amphitheatre, known as Broadway, follows one of the main streets of the Roman fortress, the *via principalis*. There would have been a row of officers' houses on the left, behind the stone wall, and the barracks of the first cohort under the field on the right. Where the modern road opens out as it approaches the amphitheatre, the *via principalis* passed through one of the fortress gates before continuing down through the civilian settlement outsde the walls to quays and wharfs on the river Usk. The gateway stood mid-way along one of the four sides of the fortress defences.

Turning around at this point, and looking back along Broadway towards the museum, the visitor will gain some impression of the size of the legionary fortress as whole. To the right, behind the amphitheatre, the fortress wall continues down to the southern angle of the defences. To the left, a grassy scarp on a tree line marks the line of the now vanished wall as it ran towards the Prysg Field barracks at the west angle. The church tower, among the trees, stands at the centre of the fortress, over the *principia* or headquarters building. To the immediate right is the amphitheatre itself, whilst to the left, the Caerleon Rugby Club pitch is on the site of the parade ground of the Second Augustan Legion.

The Building and Appearance of the Amphitheatre

The soldiers of the legion, originally recruited from northern Italy, Provence and southern Spain, would expect, even in this remote frontier base, to be provided with some of the amenities of home. The fortress baths were, as we have seen, planned on a generous scale from the outset. Moreover, within the first generation of the fortress, another bath building was constructed outside the defences to the south-west, perhaps for the inhabitants of the settlement that catered for the needs of the soldiers, which sprang up beyond the walls.

Around AD 90, however, it was decided to provide the legion with a stone amphitheatre. Space was limited, with much of it already taken up by the civilian settlement, by storage sheds outside the walls of the fortress and by an extramural bath building. Indeed, when the amphitheatre was constructed, it was necessary to rebuild one corner of the baths to avoid blocking one of the planned entrances. The siting of the amphitheatre in this position shows that no real trouble was now expected from the Silures. It obstructs the field of fire from the fortress walls, and could have given cover to attackers.

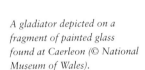

A gladiator depicted on a fragment of painted glass found at Caerleon (© National Museum of Wales).

Left: Part of the baths built outside the south-west defences of the fortress. When the amphitheatre was constructed around AD 90 this corner had to be rebuilt to avoid blocking one of the entrances to the new structure.

Opposite: An aerial view of the amphitheatre from the north (Skyscan Balloon Photography for Cadw).

An artist's impression of the Caerleon amphitheatre as it may have appeared in the late first century AD (Illustration by John Banbury, 1997, after R. A. Anderson).

Right: 'Third cohort, century of Rufinus Primus': one of the inscriptions from the amphitheatre recording the units of the legion that took part in its construction (© National Museum of Wales).

Inside and out, the amphitheatre would have looked very like a modern provincial Spanish bullring. The lower part was of stone, well buttressed to resist the pressure of the earth banking, and was never higher than we see today. The upper part was probably an open-framed timber grandstand, perhaps intended as a temporary measure, but never replaced in stone. Inside was an oval *arena* (the word means 'sand' in both Latin and Spanish) surrounded by tiers of wooden seating.

There were two major entrances or *portae pompae*, through which the procession of performers would enter the arena at the beginning of the games, saluting the president — the legionary legate or a distinguished visitor — seated in a box above one of the side entrances. Six lesser entrances were spaced around the arena and these allowed spectators to gain access to their seats and performers (animal or human) access to the central arena. The timber grandstand contained around 6,000 seats, slightly more than the full complement of the legion.

The legion's stonemasons who, with its carpenters, built the amphitheatre, recorded their work on inscribed stones naming the century responsible for a particular part of the walling. This would also serve as a form of quality control. Several of these were found during the excavations directed by Mortimer Wheeler in 1926–27, and can be seen in the displays at the National Roman Legion Museum. They begin with a symbol like a figure 7 meaning 'century of', followed by the name of the centurion, and sometimes the number of his cohort.

A Tour of the Amphitheatre

From the entrance to the site, you can walk down into the arena through the north entrance ([**F**] on plan), one of a pair of processional entries (*portae pompae*) on the long axis of the arena. The outer part of this entrance was barrel vaulted in stone, with massive dressed-stone arches at either end of the vault. The inner half was unroofed and open to the sky. The jambs of dressed freestone, which supported the vault, survive to their full height. In the opposite (southern) entrance [**B**], collapsed stones from the arch were found lying where they had fallen. Some of the Roman paving of the northern entrance survives, now protected by a rail. A large drain runs under the entrance, across the arena, and out through its southern counterpart down to the Usk. It still drains the arena very effectively in wet weather.

In Roman times, the present grass surface would have been sand or fine gravel, giving a secure foothold to the gladiators and beast hunters to whom a slipped foot would often have been fatal. Around the arena, a shallow drain carries off the surface water and behind this are the remains of the arena wall. This was once finished with a surface of smooth white plaster, painted with red lines to represent dressed ashlar. Small areas of this survived

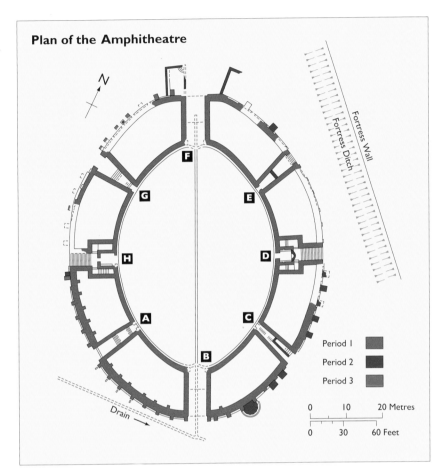

Plan of the Amphitheatre

Fortress Wall

Fortress Ditch

Period 1
Period 2
Period 3

Drain →

0   10   20 Metres

0   30   60 Feet

A general view of the amphitheatre arena looking through the northern of the main entrances or portae pompae. *A portion of the Roman paving, now protected by a rail, survives in this entrance.*

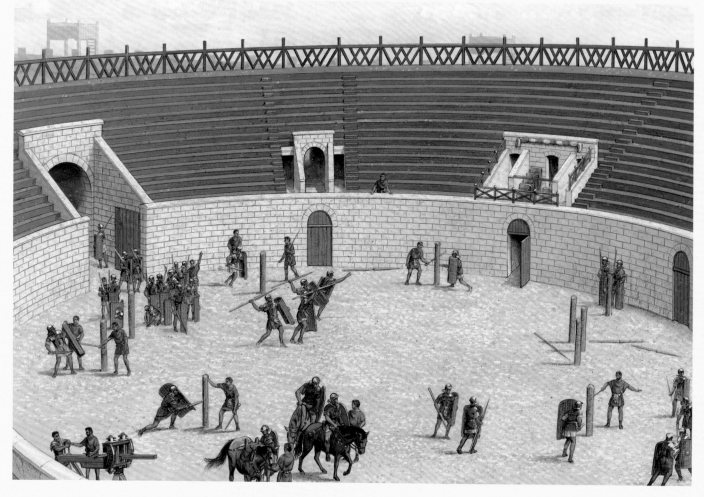

Games in the Amphitheatre

Above: In addition to the games held as part of important festivals, the amphitheatre would also have been used for regular military training and weapon demonstrations (Illustration by Peter Connolly, 1988).

Above right: This early fifth-century ivory from Rome is the left-hand leaf of a diptych. It shows a president, with two companions, presiding over an elk hunt in an amphitheatre (By courtesy of National Museums, Liverpool).

Games would usually be part of a religious or military festival, much as a saint's day may be celebrated today with a bullfight in some countries. After the hard work of a ceremonial parade to celebrate the legion's birthday (23 September), that of the emperor or those of past emperors of good repute (who were regarded as gods), the soldiers could look forward to the entertainment offered by the amphitheatre. Top gladiators were expensive, just as their present day musical or sporting counterparts are, but a 'star' name might be hired for a special occasion. There was perhaps no shortage of lesser performers or even amateurs from within the legion. Cheaper still were condemned criminals, sentenced to the beasts,

or to fight with the gladiators. Lions or leopards would rarely be seen at Caerleon, if at all, but the local forests could provide bears, wild boars or wolves, and bulls and even cows were often used in the arena. Other animals, such as deer, might be hunted on horseback in *venationes* or mounted hunts.

Of the human victims, the fullest accounts are of condemned Christians, for the endurances of these 'athletes of Christ' were recorded by their fellow believers. We have, for example, the prison diary of Vibia Perpetua, a young married woman from Carthage (in modern Tunisia), who was killed in the arena there, with a group of her fellow Christians, to celebrate the birthday of

at the time of excavation. The wall was crowned with a heavy stone coping carrying a rail. Above this, on the banking, which was never any higher than it is today, were the tiers of wooden seats; traces of the timber uprights have been found in excavation.

The spectator, with a 'ticket' (in the form of a lead token), would approach via one of the six lesser entrances, passing down a flight of stairs and up another at the side, out on to the banking where the seats were probably numbered.

The two side entrances ([D] and [H] on plan) on the short axis of the arena were larger. Each had a pair of staircases up to the terrace, flanking either side of a small, square central room that had access to the outside staircase and to the arena. Here, gladiators or prisoners would await their turn, and wild beasts would be penned before being released into the arena and the roar of the crowd. One of the staircases in entrance [D] (that on the left with the brick apse) is wider and probably led up to a private box above the entrance itself. Entrance [H] also had a private box above. These boxes provided seating for the president of the games and various officials and important guests.

During the history of the fortress, the amphitheatre was repaired from time to time. The external buttresses were rebuilt or renewed and the spaces at the bottom of all the entrances

The outside wall of the amphitheatre was strongly buttressed to resist the thrust of the earth fill. These buttresses were rebuilt or renewed from time to time during the history of the amphitheatre.

emperor Geta in AD 203. There is no evidence, however, that any Christian martyrs suffered in the Caerleon amphitheatre. The two Caerleon martyrs, Julius and Aaron, if legionaries (and therefore Roman citizens), would have been beheaded rather than subjected to the sadistic indignities of the arena.

The amphitheatre could also be used for military training or weapon demonstrations, and as a place where the legion could be assembled for a speech from its commander or a visiting dignitary. It is no coincidence that it stood next to the parade ground, which would have had a saluting base for similar, but more formal occasions.

*The side entrance [**H**], which includes a chamber or pen from which performers would be released into the arena.*

Repairs to the amphitheatre were undertaken during the reign of the emperor Caracalla (AD 211–17). His likeness appears on this coin — a type nicknamed the antoninianus, *which was introduced in AD 215 (© National Museum of Wales).*

except the *portae pompae* were filled in, thereby burying the lower parts of the steps (this filling has now been removed). Entrances [**D**] and [**H**] on the short axis were altered more radically.

Entrance [**H**], on the right, is very well preserved. At the bottom of the entrance steps, the brick arch under which spectators turned right to reach the steps up to the seating still survives. So, too, does a large block of stone, originally from the barrel vault of the entrance, which was carefully set into the angle of the passage during later alterations, perhaps for a steward or ticket collector. The left-hand stair (looking into the amphitheatre) was blocked and filled at the same time.

The brick rear wall of the beast pen, or waiting room for gladiators, which opens on to the arena also survives. The line of its original barrel vault and door can be seen marked on the brickwork, together with the line of a later altered doorway. During the renovations in the early third century, under Septimius Severus or Caracalla (p. 12), the entrance was filled in level with the ground outside, burying and so preserving the earlier features we can see today.

Directly opposite, entrance [**D**] also shows evidence of alterations. Here, the broad stair, which probably led to the president's box, was blocked and filled in. The

entry from the staircase to the small chamber for wild beasts or gladiators was also blocked, so that this could now only be reached from the arena; a cupboard-like feature was inserted in its rear wall. Later, as with entrance [**H**], this entry was filled in level with the surrounding ground and the brick niche was inserted in the rear wall of the chamber. On excavation, many of its bricks were found to be stamped LEG II AVG ANTO, using the title 'Antoninus's (Caracalla's) Own' held by the legion from AD 212–22.

In these later phases, this chamber may have been used as a shrine to Nemesis, the goddess of fate and divine vengeance, who punished crime. Shrines to Nemesis are known at other amphitheatres, including Chester. Here, at Caerleon, a lead plaque found in the arena carries a scratched dedication to the goddess, asking for a curse on an unnamed person. The story behind this is not wholly clear, but it was common for the victim of a theft to dedicate either the stolen object, or the thief, to a god or goddess in return for vengeance. In this case, a cloak and a pair of boots were involved and the writer of the curse, who may have been a gladiator, seems to be wishing ill upon the (? unknown) thief, whom he perhaps suspected was another gladiator — 'May he not redeem them, save with his life blood'.

Leaving the amphitheatre by the main south entrance ([B] on plan), you will notice the massive freestone piers supporting the vault over its outer half, still standing to almost their full height.

Turning right, and returning towards the site entrance, we may observe the well-preserved buttressed exterior. Stone slabs, set like bollards, can be seen near some of the buttresses. These were placed to prevent damage by vehicles using the perimeter road. Near entrance [H], the furnace and a corner of the large first-century bath building can be seen. The building predated the amphitheatre but was remodelled when the latter was built so that it did not block the adjacent entrance or the perimeter road.

You should now leave the site and return to Broadway, to the point where the modern road broadens out as it approaches the amphitheatre car park.

Left: 'To the goddess Nemesis, I give this cloak and these boots…': a lead curse tablet found near the eastern entrance [D] (© National Museum of Wales).

Below: The eastern entrance to the amphitheatre [D], with the later brick apse of the shrine of Nemesis. The president's box was probably located above.

The South-West Defences

The modern road outside the amphitheatre is on the line of the Roman road from the south-west gate of the fortress to the river. On the right, behind the amphitheatre, the line of the Roman defences can be seen as a low, stone wall, with higher ground to its rear. The wall runs down from near the road to the southern angle of the fortress. It has been much robbed for building stone in past centuries. The squared blocks of sandstone with which it was once faced are now mostly gone, leaving the rubble core exposed.

Originally, the defences comprised a turf and clay bank crowned with timber defences, a timber gate with twin towers flanking a central entrance, and possibly a series of timber towers at spaced intervals (see illustrations, pp. 15–16). Later, at the beginning of the second century AD, these timber defences were replaced by a stone wall 5 feet (1.5m) thick fronting the original bank (now represented by the higher ground inside the wall), a twin-towered stone gate and a series of stone turrets at intervals of about 46 yards (43m).

Where the modern road broadens out as it approaches the amphitheatre, the south-west gate spanned the Roman road out of the fortress. Of its two flanking towers, that on the left has been excavated (though nothing is visible today). It projected from the line of the wall, and may have been remodelled in the early third century, for an inscription of Caracalla (AD 211–17) was found nearby in 1603. The right-hand tower lies under the small walled yard by the roadside and awaits excavation.

Opposite: An aerial view showing the early second-century wall at the south-western corner of the fortress. Its present state is due to stone robbing, rather than purely age.

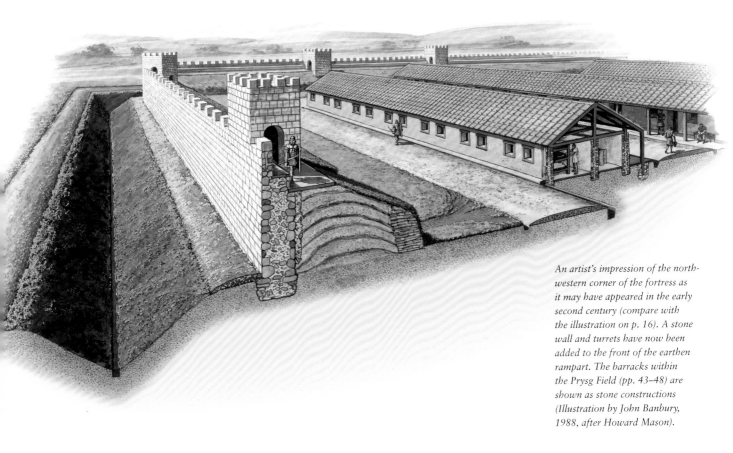

An artist's impression of the north-western corner of the fortress as it may have appeared in the early second century (compare with the illustration on p. 16). A stone wall and turrets have now been added to the front of the earthen rampart. The barracks within the Prysg Field (pp. 43–48) are shown as stone constructions (Illustration by John Banbury, 1988, after Howard Mason).

Above: At its southern angle, the fortress wall stands to a height of some 12 feet (3.5m). The holes used to support the scaffolding during construction can still be seen, as can a brick-arched drain that once discharged into the ditch.

Right: The basement of one of the series of turrets that guarded the fortress wall. The front wall of this turret has been removed in antiquity by stone robbers.

A Tour of the Defences

From the road follow the fortress wall down to its southern angle. Until quite recently, the Roman wall was partly hidden by Victorian facing. This has now been removed and the Roman stonework conserved. Of the three internal turrets along this stretch of wall, two are unexcavated. Their positions are known, but the evidence they contain has been left intact for the future. The wall in front of the third turret has been entirely robbed out, exposing the interior.

The towers were of two storeys, the lower being a basement built into the bank and serving only to support the floor above. The ground floor of the excavated tower was reached through a door in its rear wall and was used, perhaps illicitly, for dumping ashes and rubbish from the cooking ovens to the rear. When found, it was filled with 5 feet (1.5m) of ashes and clay, rich in occupation debris. In the mid-second century, a cookhouse, like those to be seen in the Prysg Field (pp. 43–44), was added behind. This has not, however, been excavated and the doorway to the rear of the turret has been blocked off, with a datestone to show that this is modern masonry.

Inside the southern angle, the corner turret, originally excavated in 1909, has been exposed and conserved. The legion's masons had trouble with the wall here owing to subsidence. Several settlement cracks can be seen on the outside of the wall, which shows substantial signs of rebuilding. Inside the angle was a latrine, like that in the Prysg Field, but this is not now visible. This corner of the fortress was used in World War II for a brick Home Guard rifle position, covering the bridge, but regrettably it has been necessary to remove this relic of more recent history in order to conserve the Roman wall.

The wall itself still stands to a height of around 12 feet (3.5m) at the rounded southern angle, though it is necessary to retrace one's steps to see this impressive work from outside. As elsewhere, the facework has been robbed, but the brick fragments and the crushed brick in the mortar show where it has been rebuilt in Roman times. A number of 'putlog' holes for the wooden scaffolding or staging used to build the wall can be seen, and just past the angle is a brick-arched drain, from the inside of the fortress, which originally discharged into the ditch. Beyond, another interval turret is just visible.

Leaving the defences in this southern corner of the fortress, you can return to the road near the amphitheatre and follow the footpath on the opposite side to the Prysg Field barracks, or follow the footpath across the field and return up the main street to the fortress baths.

Outside the Walls: The Civilian Settlements

Nothing is now visible of the crowded civilian settlements — *canabae* — that lay outside the fortress, housing the many merchants, craftsmen and camp followers who accompanied the legion. This community would have had a profound effect on the local economy, supplying goods and services to the resident garrison. Also present were the soldiers' dependants, including wives — official or otherwise — and the families of serving legionaries and veterans.

The main concentrations of settlement lay to the south-west and north-east of the fortress, though inscriptions also refer to temples of Diana and Mithras, perhaps indicating an as yet unlocated temple quarter. There were also several extramural bath buildings, which no doubt served the civilian population as well as the soldiers, who were already well provided for with the fortress bathhouse.

To the south-west of the fortress, behind the amphitheatre and parade ground, was an area that appears to have been relatively high in status, with a row of stone buildings, possibly shops and houses, and a large courtyard building, which may have been a *mansio* or guest house for official travellers. Beyond, a large unexcavated area of settlement lies under the present golf course, leading to the Roman quays at the bottom of Broadway. In contrast, north-east of the fortress, the Mill Street settlement seems to have been a relatively low-status suburb of fairly small rectangular houses standing in a pattern of streets, perhaps occupied by soldiers' families.

There was a further suburb across the river Usk, *'Ultra Pontem'*, and a small settlement at nearby Bulmore. The recovery of tombstones of legionary veterans in these districts suggests that they may have been quiet residential areas mainly for retired people.

Although there are no visible traces of the cemeteries that lay along the roads leading from the fortress, many cremations, burials and tombstones have been recovered, which provide some insight into the mixed population that occupied the fortress and its environs.

The civilian settlements that clustered around the legionary fortress contained not only houses, but also the shops and workshops of craftsmen necessary to sustain the population. This Gallo-Roman relief shows a customer at a wine merchant's shop (Musée Archeologique, Dijon; photo: AKG Images/ Erich Lessing).

Left: A stone relief of Cornelius Castus and his wife, Julia Belismicus, shown sacrificing to Fortune (Fortuna) and Good Luck (Bonus Eventus) from the 'Castle' baths outside the fortress. Fortuna often figured in bathhouse dedications, since it was thought that a naked man was vulnerable to evil forces and needed protection (© National Museum of Wales).

Below: Many veterans of Legio II Augusta settled near the fortress. This tombstone from Great Bulmore commemorates one such veteran, Julius Valens, who died at the age of 100 (© National Museum of Wales).

The Prysg Field Barracks

From the footpath, the grassy scarp you see on the tree line to the right marks the vanished defences. The broad hollow in front of this is on the line of the ditch, but its profile bears no relationship to the actual Roman ditch. A gravel path over this hollow leads, through a gate, to the Prysg Field barracks.

Victor Nash-Williams's excavations here in 1927–29 uncovered a row of barrack buildings, each of which had housed a legionary century, with its centurion. Similar barracks have been excavated in various parts of the Roman empire, but these are the only legionary barrack blocks now visible in Europe. As its name implies, each century at one time comprised 100 men, but by the time *Isca* was established the complement had become 80. A century was divided into ten groups of eight men, each group sharing a pair of rooms in the barrack block. This arrangement was derived from conditions on campaign, when eight men would share a rectangular tent, the tents of each century being pitched in a line, with the larger tent of the centurion and his staff at the end.

The centuries, or infantry companies, were grouped into cohorts, or battalions, each of about 500 men — six centuries of 80 men apiece, making a total of 480. There were ten cohorts in the legion, so that 60 barrack blocks of the type seen in the Prysg Field would be needed for the entire legion (bearing in mind the complications with the first cohort, see p. 7). Ten groups of barrack blocks can be identified in the plan of *Isca*, with all save those of the first cohort comprising six barracks. Four groups of six were located in the front range of the fortress, and four in the rear. The two remaining cohorts, including the first, were housed each side of the headquarters building in the central zone.

The Defences, Ovens and Cookhouses

Immediately inside the entrance gate, you will see that the Prysg Field barracks are situated within the north-western angle of the fortress. Before turning to consider the details, there are several features along the line of the defences that repay examination.

From the gate, the earthen rampart of the defences runs down towards the angle. The wall in front of it has been entirely robbed out. The space between the rampart and the perimeter road (the *via sagularis*) was used for cooking, and a number of circular oven bases can be seen. There is a stone tower, like that behind the amphitheatre, mid-way between the gate and the

Opposite: The four barrack blocks in the Prysg Field, seen from the air (Skyscan Balloon Photography for Cadw).

Far left: A first-century AD relief of two soldiers from the legionary fortress in Mainz, Germany. The figure in front carries the shaft of a standard, the top of which is now missing (Römisch-Germanische Zentralmuseum, Mainz; photo: AKG Images/Erich Lessing).

Left: The bases of circular ovens, used by the legionaries for cooking rations, situated in the Prysg Field.

Above: The silver tip of a vexillum (a legionary banner). Each century would also have had its own standard or signum (© National Museum of Wales).

Below: An artist's impression of a section through a legionary barrack block. The inner room slept eight, with arms and equipment stored in the outer room (Illustration by John Banbury, 1988, after Howard Mason).

angle, with another in the far corner. Both of these towers had cookhouses added behind them in the mid-second century. These have raised platforms inside, probably the bases for ovens and cooking hearths. To their rear, the broad *via sagularis* or perimeter road was designed to give rapid access to the ramparts, should the need arise, as well as to facilitate the movements of bodies of troops. A drain separates this road from the first of the barrack blocks.

'Single Men in Barracks': The Legionary Barrack Blocks

Only the first barrack block is of original Roman masonry. The others, at a higher level, are in effect 'plans in stone' — replicas of the original buildings have been built above them. The method of excavation used in 1927–29 merely trenched the buildings, leaving much of the Roman deposits inside them intact. It was impossible to clear these for conservation without destroying the deposits, which may hold important clues for our future understanding of Caerleon. When first built, the barracks

were of timber, but wood rots rapidly in this damp soil. They were later rebuilt in stone.

The six barrack blocks of each cohort faced inwards in pairs, corresponding to the maniples or double centuries into which the cohort was divided for some purposes. The blocks are long narrow buildings with twelve pairs of rooms, each pair housing eight men, with a covered veranda running down the inner side of each block. At the far (north-west) end is the larger block of rooms housing the centurion. In theory, only ten pairs of rooms should be needed for the 80 men, but there are usually more. The extra rooms may have been needed for recruits or replacements on temporary secondment, or for *immunes* (clerks or craftsmen exempt from routine military chores because of their jobs) attached to the century for ration purposes. There may have been various reasons why the actual strength of the century sometimes varied from its establishment strength of 80.

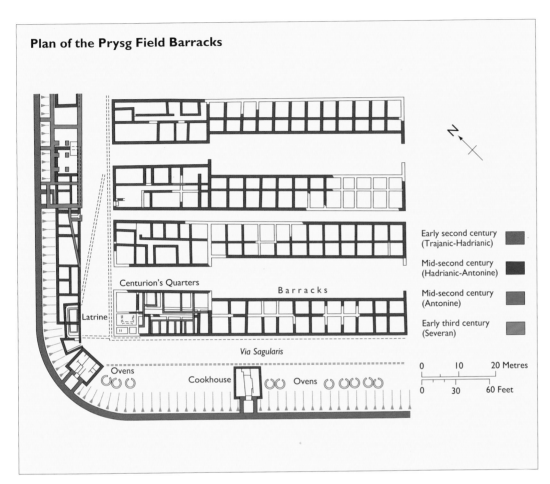

Plan of the Prysg Field Barracks

Centurion's Quarters

B a r r a c k s

Latrine

Via Sagularis

Ovens   Cookhouse   Ovens

Early second century
(Trajanic-Hadrianic)

Mid-second century
(Hadrianic-Antonine)

Mid-second century
(Antonine)

Early third century
(Severan)

0	10	20 Metres
0	30	60 Feet

*Below: Marcus Favonius Facilis,
a centurion of the Twentieth
Legion, depicted on his
tombstone from Colchester.
He is seen in full dress uniform,
with a vine stick in his hand.
The stick served as both a badge
of office and an instrument
of punishment (By courtesy
of Colchester Museums).*

Of the pairs of rooms, the outer (smaller) one would be used for storing kit, and the inner, slightly larger, for sleeping. They would have been less cramped than it might appear. Army documents surviving from elsewhere in the empire show that many men would be on detached duty — perhaps pursuing thieves, escorting tax collectors or serving in the provincial governor's bodyguard. Those in barracks would be allocated daily jobs, such as guard duty, cookhouse fatigues, cutting stone or timber, amid a variety of other jobs. It was not unknown for centurions to take bribes from soldiers who wished to avoid the dirty or unpleasant jobs. In March AD 107, for example, Julius Apollinaris — a legionary serving in the east — wrote home to his mother: 'thanks be to Serapis that while the others are working hard all day breaking stones, I am now a company clerk and stand around all day doing nothing'. He implied that money had changed hands.

'The Backbone of the Army': The Centurion and His Quarters

The ten to a dozen rooms of the centurion's suite contrast with the meagre pair in which eight of his men had to live. However, it also served as a company office and provided accommodation for the junior NCOs of the century. Tombstones of centurions show them in full regimentals, with their medals (or the Roman equivalents) up and carrying the vine stick which was their badge of office. 'Among the Romans', wrote a Greek historian, 'the vine branch is a mark of honour. And those who obtain it... become centurions'. It was, however, more than a simple badge of office and was used freely on the backs of lazy or unfortunate soldiers.

A bronze plaque depicting a winged Victory, with a trophy over her shoulder. It is possibly a fragment of parade armour or perhaps decoration from a portable shrine. It was found in the excavation of a centurion's residence at the Prysg Field (© National Museum of Wales).

Below left: Part of a record of soldiers collecting timber for building work, written in ink on a wooden tablet (© National Museum of Wales).

Below right: The centurion's suite in the first of the Prysg Field barrack blocks. Each suite had ten to twelve rooms, serving as a company office as well as the centurion's quarters.

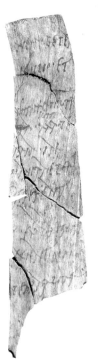

Many centurions would spend their military career in *Il Augusta*, or in the other two British legions, but others might be transferred from Britain to the legions of the Rhine, the Danube, or any other part of the empire where troops were needed. Equally, at any time, centurions might be posted to Caerleon from legions serving on the other frontiers of the Roman world.

The centurion's block may have looked not unlike a small modern office suite, with a row of rooms leading off a central corridor, and a latrine at the end. In the first barrack, the block was rebuilt later in its history and several periods of work are now visible.

The overall plan can be better appreciated, without this complication, by examining one of the three barrack blocks situated at the higher level.

The occupants were no strangers to paperwork — daily rosters, ration receipts, pay records and the like all had to be dealt with. For this, they employed carefully prepared shavings of wood, not unlike file cards in general format (for paper did not reach the west, from China, before the later Middle Ages), on which they wrote in ink. Waxed tablets were also used for other purposes. A surviving ink record on part of a wooden tablet from Caerleon lists men collecting timber for building work. From elsewhere, both in Britain and the east, virtual archives survive, recording in detail many aspects of the daily life of the men of the Roman army.

The Latrine

In the western angle of the fortress, next to the corner turret, is a latrine. Built about AD 150, an earlier rampart building was demolished to make way for it. The remains are those of a single rectangular room (the foundation across the middle belongs to the earlier building), with a drain around three sides of the interior. Over the drain there would have been a series of wooden seats, but we should not imagine any partitions or separate cubicles. In front of the drain is a gutter in which the legionaries would have washed the sponges that served them for lavatory paper. The sponges, on sticks, would have been rinsed in a tub of vinegar on the floor. The small room to one side probably housed a water tank and the flushing arrangements.

The North-West Rampart Buildings

On the far side of the Prysg Field along the back of the rampart, behind the centurions' quarters, a further series of buildings is known from excavation, though nothing is now visible. In the early second century there were originally six blocks (with two pairs built end to end) serving the twelve centuries. This represents one per double century, with a mess-room or stores for one century at each end, two smaller rooms, and a central lobby. Similar mess-blocks or quartermaster's stores are known from elsewhere in *Isca*, and at the legionary fortress at Chester. At *Isca*, in the third century, these blocks were replaced by a continuous range of magazines or stores, some with what were probably the bases for raised tanks to collect rainwater from the roofs.

When excavated, the buildings contained quantities of weapons and military equipment, including chain mail, lance heads and spear heads, many arrowheads and *pilum* heads from long-stemmed javelins, which were characteristic weapons of the legionary soldier. There were iron caltrops — vicious spiked objects that could be strewn on the ground to lame both men and horses, sword fittings of bone and bronze, and in one room someone had been making and repairing the composite bows with which archers in some army units were equipped under the late empire.

Left: The latrine in the western angle of the fortress, at the Prysg Field barracks.

Below: An artist's reconstruction of the Prysg Field latrine. The form of the wooden seats is known from surviving marble examples at Mediterranean sites (Illustration by John Banbury, 1988, after Howard Mason).

The legionary barracks in Prysg Field, which were excavated by Victor Nash-Williams of the National Museum of Wales in 1927–29.

Caltrops were scattered on the ground to lame men and horses. This is one of many found during the excavations of the north-west rampart buildings in Prysg Field (© National Museum of Wales).

Further Reading

Acknowledgements

The author and Cadw are grateful to Richard Brewer, J. David Zienkiewicz and David M. Robinson for their help in compiling this guidebook and the previous edition on which it is closely based.

C. J. Arnold and J. L. Davies, *Roman and Early Medieval Wales* (Stroud 2000).

G. C. Boon, Isca: *The Roman Legionary Fortress at Caerleon, Mon.*, third edition (Cardiff 1972) is the standard work, now updated by Boon, *The Legionary Fortress at Caerleon–Isca: A Brief Account* (Cardiff 1987).

R. J. Brewer, *Caerleon–Isca: The Roman Legionary Museum* (Cardiff 1987), revised as *Caerleon and the Roman Army* (Cardiff 2002).

R. J. Brewer (ed.) *The Second Augustan Legion and the Roman Military Machine* (Cardiff 2002).

D. R. Evans and V. M. Metcalf, *Roman Gates, Caerleon*, Oxbow Monograph 15 (Oxford 1992).

Edith Evans, *The Caerleon Canabae: Excavations in the Civil Settlement 1984–90*, Britannia Monograph Series No. 16 (London 2000).

R. G. Collingwood and R. P. Wright, *The Roman Inscriptions of Britain*, vol i (Oxford 1965), where the inscriptions from Caerleon are collected.

T. Copeland, *Caerleon–Isca: An Educational Resource Pack* (Cardiff 1997).

M. G. Jarrett, 'Legio II Augusta in Britain', *Archaeologia Cambrensis* **113** (1964), 47–63.

W. Manning, *Roman Wales* (Cardiff 2001).

V. E. Nash-Williams, 'The Roman Legionary Fortress at Caerleon in Monmouthshire: Report on the Excavations carried out in the Prysg Field', *Archaeologia Cambrensis* **86** (1931), 99–157 and **87** (1932), 48–104, 265–349.

V. E. Nash-Williams, *The Roman Frontier in Wales*, second edition, revised by M. G. Jarrett (Cardiff 1969).

E. A. M. Shirley, *Building a Roman Fortress* (Stroud 2001).

G. Webster, *The Roman Imperial Army*, third edition (London 1985).

R. E. M. Wheeler and T. V. Wheeler, 'The Roman Amphitheatre at Caerleon', *Archaeologia* **78** (1928), 111–218.

J. David Zienkiewicz, *The Legionary Fortress Baths at Caerleon*, 2 vols (Cardiff 1986).

J. David Zienkiewicz, *Roman Gems from Caerleon* (Cardiff 1987).

J. David Zienkiewicz, *Roman Legion* (Cardiff 1994, reprinted 2002).